EYEWITNESS READERS

PROFICIENT 4 READERS

HORSE HEROES

TRUE STORIES
OF AMAZING HORSES

Written by Kate Petty

DK

DORLING KINDERSLEY
London • New York • Sydney • Moscow
www.dk.com

Horses in history

People and horses have always had a special relationship. Ever since horses were first tamed and ridden 6,000 years ago, they have been admired for their intelligence, strength and speed.

In ancient Greece, a beautiful, well-trained horse was the ultimate status symbol of kings and generals. The conqueror Alexander the Great was so proud of his brave horse Bucephalus (Bew-seff-a-lus), that he named a city after him.

Pegasus
In Greek mythology, Pegasus was a beautiful winged horse who became a constellation of stars in the sky.

This statue shows Alexander the Great riding Bucephalus into battle.

This is a bronze model of a Roman racing chariot called a biga. Bigas were pulled by two-horse teams.

Chariots
Roman chariot races were dangerous and exciting. Crashes were common, but horses could race on without a charioteer.

Citizens of the Roman Empire loved the drama of horse racing. They flocked to the arena to watch their favourite chariot teams thundering around the racetrack.

Horses were also important to Native Americans. The tribes of the Great Plains were expert horsemen and relied on horses for carrying them into battle and for hunting buffalo.

Wherever people and horses have worked together, they have formed a loyal bond. This book tells the stories of some remarkable horses that have worked with their human partners to become heroes.

Roman racers
Champion stallions were used for breeding during their racing years.

Saddlebag art
Horses were very important to the Native American Dakota (Sioux) tribe. They were a favourite theme in Dakota art.

Pony Express

When the little mustang came into view that warm April evening in 1860, the crowd began to clap and cheer.

Her rider, Johnny Fry, led her into the packed town square of St Joseph, Missouri. Johnny checked the mail pouch on the mustang's back for the last time as she snorted and stamped in anticipation.

Long journey
Pony Express riders took the mail 3,200 kilometres (2,000 miles) from Missouri to California in the United States (USA).

This poster for the Pony Express service dates from 1861.

First delivery
Johnny Fry's mail sack held 49 letters and 3 newspapers.

The cost of sending a letter by Pony Express was worked out by weight. A letter cost $5 per 28 grams (about £100 in today's money).

A cannon boomed. They were away! The mustang raced off into the evening twilight, leaving the cheering crowds far behind.

Horse and rider had entered history as the first ever Pony Express team.

In 1860 there were no such things as telephones and fax machines. If you lived on the west coast of the United States, it was almost impossible to keep up with the latest news on the east coast. It could take more than a month for mail to travel across the continent by wagon.

The Pony Express was designed to improve that – cutting down the time taken to just eight days. Horses and riders ran in continuous relays so that the mail was kept moving day and night.

Mustang
This hardy breed is descended from the horses brought to America by Spanish explorers.

Express riders
Pony Express riders had to be under 18 years old and weigh less than 57 kilograms (126 pounds), so that the horses were not slowed down.

Each horse and rider galloped at top speed to the next station. The rider leapt off the exhausted horse shouting "Pony rider coming!" The mail was transferred to a fresh horse and the rider galloped off again on his new mount.

Transfer
It took a rider two minutes to transfer between horses.

Saddle up
Mail pouches were sometimes sewn into the rider's saddle.

There were 157 relay stations and a rider would change horses about six to eight times along his particular stretch of the route.

Express riders carried rifles in case of trouble.

Horse and rider teams risked death together daily.

Much of the route lay through the homelands of Native Americans, who attacked the white invaders of their territory.

One of the bravest riders was "Pony Bob" Haslam. In May 1860 he arrived at a station in Nevada to find the keeper dead and all the horses gone. He set out for the next station which was 64 kilometres (40 miles) away.

"I knew I had to carry on. As I rode through the night, I kept watching my pony's ears. I knew he'd hear any Indian ambush before I did."

At the next station he persuaded the keeper to leave with them. He and his tireless horse saved the man's life – the next night, that station was attacked.

Quiver contains about 20 arrows

Strap for slinging bow and quiver across back

Lethal weapon
Several riders were wounded by arrows. This bow, quiver and arrows comes from the Dakota (Sioux) tribe.

Lincoln
In 1860, Abraham Lincoln's first speech as president of the USA was carried by the Pony Express.

Stagecoach
When the Pony Express closed, Wells, Fargo & Company ran stagecoaches along the route. Stagecoaches took about 25 days to reach California.

The Pony Express teams rode across rocky mountain passes and wide, empty plains in all kinds of weather. They faced scorching sun, torrential rain and blizzards. If their rider fell off, some horses carried on alone to the next station.

The final stop was Sacramento, California. Crowds of people, eager to receive their mail and newspapers from the east, would gather to watch the arrival of the last horse and rider on the route.

Despite its popularity, the Pony Express was closed down in 1861. Once the telegraph system was completed, there was no need for an express postal service. But the horses and riders went down in history for their daring mail runs. Whatever the dangers the riders encountered along the way, they kept their promise that "the mail must get through". ❖

Tschiffely
Aimé Tschiffely
(Ay-may
Shiff-ell-ee)
was a Swiss
teacher living
in Argentina.

Americas
Tschiffely
wanted to ride
all the way
from South to
North America.

Tale of two horses

When Tschiffely told people about his idea early in 1925, they thought he had gone mad.

"Impossible! It can't be done!"

Tschiffely wanted to be the first person ever to ride from Buenos Aires in Argentina all the way to Washington in the United States.

He realized that the 16,000-kilometre (10,000-mile) journey would be full of difficulties, but it had been his ambition for years.

Tschiffely needed two tough horses if he was to succeed. He chose Gato and Mancha. They were Criollo horses aged 15 and 16 that had belonged to an Argentinian Indian chief. They were used to roaming free on the plains and knew how to survive in the wild.

Tschiffely and the horses set off in April 1925.

After four months, the trio reached Bolivia. By this time they had learnt to trust each other and to work as a team.

They travelled along the shore of Lake Titicaca and crossed into Peru. As they rode over a wide plain, they came to a shallow strip of water. Gato suddenly reared up and refused to go on.

Then a man rushed towards them, shouting that they must not cross. He said that the water hid dangerous quicksands that would suck them under. Tschiffely was amazed. Gato had saved their lives.

Criollo
These horses are very tough and can carry heavy weights over long distances.

Alert
People believe that horses have a sixth sense that warns them about danger.

Andes
The Andes reach over 6,000 metres (20,000 feet). They are pitted with sheer, rocky gorges.

Rope bridge
Andes natives have built thin rope bridges across gorges for centuries. Many people have to be blindfolded and strapped on to stretchers to cross them.

As they rode on through Peru, they began to climb the Andes – a huge range of snow-capped mountains.

One morning, Tschiffely came across a sight that made his blood run cold. The only way forward was a rickety old rope bridge that stretched over a deep gorge. One slip would be fatal.

Slowly, Tschiffely and Mancha began to cross. Tschiffely spoke to his horse in a quiet, calm voice, gently patting Mancha's haunches.

Halfway across, the bridge began to sway violently. If Mancha panicked and turned back they would both fall to their deaths. But Mancha waited calmly for the bridge to stop moving, then carried on. When Gato saw his companions safe on the other side, he crossed the bridge as steadily as if he were walking on solid ground.

Broken trail
Constant rain
in mountainous
regions often
washes away
part of the
hillside in a
landslide.

From Peru, Tschiffely headed into
Ecuador and followed a series of
tracks through lush forests, over high
mountains and down into valleys.

At night, Tschiffely never tethered the horses. He knew they would not stray. The three travellers were sharing the great adventure, each showing the others the way.

Zigzagging up a narrow trail one day, Tschiffely saw that the path ahead had been swept away by a landslide, leaving a sheer drop. There was no choice but to turn back and find another route. Tschiffely tightened Gato's packs ready for a long detour.

But Mancha had other ideas. Tschiffely saw with horror that Mancha was preparing to jump the gap. His heart was in his mouth as Mancha sailed through the air and landed on the other side. The horse turned and neighed to his companions. Gato soon followed him. Last to jump was Tschiffely.

Herd instincts
Wild horses live in groups, or herds. They form strong bonds and Mancha and Gato would instinctively follow each other, whatever the dangers.

High jump
Horses push off to jump from their back legs. Mancha was particularly brave, as the ground was so slippery.

17

Dense jungle
The jungles of Central America are home to some of the world's most dangerous snakes, such as the 9-metre (30-foot) anaconda.

Crocodiles
Horses seem to remember that their ancestors were hunted by crocodiles, and know they are to be feared.

At last the travellers reached Panama, the narrow country that links North and South America.

From here they journeyed on into Costa Rica, trekking through dense jungle. All three were bitten by mosquitoes and they were constantly on the alert for poisonous snakes.

Once, Mancha slipped into a crocodile-infested river. Just in time, he managed to find a foothold and scramble up the bank, while Tschiffely clung on for dear life.

Two and a half years after setting out from Buenos Aires, Tschiffely reached Washington. He had achieved his ambition.

"I could never have done it," he said, "without Mancha and Gato. My two pals have shown powers of resistance to every hardship."

Tschiffely was given a hero's welcome and met President Coolidge at the White House. Admirers suggested that the horses should live in a city park. But Tschiffely took Mancha and Gato back to Argentina and set them free. ❖

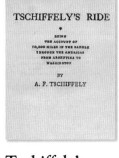

Tschiffely's Ride
Now a famous man, Aimé Tschiffely wrote a book about his adventures.

Born free
Horses that grow up in the country can pine away if confined in a city. They need to be able to roam free in open pasture.

Movie town
The 1930s saw
the golden age
of film making
in Hollywood,
California.

Hollywood hero

In 1932 a star was born.
He was a beautiful golden
colour with a white, flowing
mane and tail. Bred from a
palomino mare and a racehorse,
Golden Cloud was to become the
most famous horse of his day.

Golden Cloud made his big
screen debut in 1938. His owners,
Hudkin Stables, hired
him out to play a part
in the Hollywood film
*The Adventures of
Robin Hood*.

Later that year, a
major film studio
decided to make a series of
Westerns featuring Roy
Rogers, the singing cowboy actor.
They brought several horses round
for Roy to audition. He fell for
Golden Cloud the moment he
climbed on to the horse's back.

First part
In the film *The
Adventures of
Robin Hood*,
Golden Cloud
played Maid
Marion's trusty
steed, complete
with medieval
costume.

Roy Rogers was called the King of the Cowboys, and Trigger soon became known as the "smartest horse in the movies".

Famous pose
Trigger's most spectacular feat was rearing up on his back legs with Roy Rogers on his back.

While they were making their first film, *Under Western Stars*, Golden Cloud was renamed "Trigger" because he was so quick.

Roy loved Trigger so much that, after completing three films, he bought him for $2,500. Roy and Trigger became full-time partners.

Expensive
Trigger was a true Hollywood horse. His silver saddle cost $50,000 and was set with 1,000 rubies.

Starring role
One of Trigger's best-loved movies was *Under California Stars* made in 1948. In this film, Trigger is stolen by thugs.

Trigger loved the camera. He often stole the show from Roy Rogers with a well-timed yawn or dance step.

He knew more than 60 tricks. He could walk 150 steps on his hind legs, stamp his hoof to count and draw a gun from a holster.

Trigger became one of the most popular characters in show business. He starred in 87 films and 101 TV shows, and once he even had a party in the Grand Ballroom of the Astor Hotel in New York.

Trigger presents his passport for inspection on arrival in England in 1954.

Like a true star, Trigger made special personal appearances. He always travelled in style, carried his own horse-sized passport and signed his name with an X in hotel registers.

Trigger finally retired from show business in 1957 and died in 1965, aged 33. Roy Rogers was heartbroken. He had lost "the greatest horse who ever came along". ❖

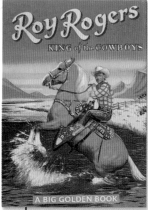

Fan club
Trigger's fan club produced hundreds of books and toys for its members.

AUSTRIA • Vienna
• Piber Stud Farm

Vienna
The Spanish Riding School of Vienna, Austria, was founded in 1572. It is called "Spanish" because the original horses in the School were from Spain.

Ballet on horseback

"He's a lively one," said the stable lad, pointing towards the dark colt leading the race across the field.

The colt's name was Favory. He was one of the Lipizzaner foals born in the early 1980s at the Piber Stud Farm, where horses are bred for the Spanish Riding School.

Lipizzaner horses and foals run free on the Piber Stud Farm.

"Look how much energy he's got," said the stable lad.

"Maybe too much," said one of the grooms. Favory was popular at the stud farm, but could he make it at the School? The groom knew that to become one of the horses that perform at the School's regular displays, a horse had to have personality, discipline and strength.

Lipizzaner
The School's horses are Lipizzaners. They are all descended from six stallions, one of which was named Favory. His descendants are always given his name.

Lipizzaner foals are born dark but usually turn white when they are two years old.

Arena
The grand Winter Riding Hall was built in 1735 by Emperor Charles VI of Austria. His portrait hangs at the far end of the arena.

When Favory was three and a half years old it was time to begin his training.

He travelled with the other new students to Vienna. Here in the School's Winter Riding Hall, horses train and perform dressage, a set of complicated steps which have been the same for centuries. The School is famous worldwide for the skill with which its horses can do dressage.

Hardest of all the steps are the "Airs above the ground", a series of amazing jumps that only the strongest horses can perform.

Everyone was anxious to see if any of the new students looked strong and steady enough to make the grade.

Unfortunately, Favory didn't give a very good first impression. He broke away from his groom, trotted down the ramp and galloped around the hall, showing off.

"We've got our work cut out with that one," said one of the riders. Watching Favory very closely was the First Chief Rider, the most experienced rider in the School. He liked horses with spirit. But did Favory have the self-control that he would need to perform the Airs?

There was only one way to find out for sure.

Riders
Riders join the school as teenagers and train for six years. A Chief Rider must have taught at least one horse the Airs.

Costume
Riders perform wearing cocked hats, smart tailcoats and high black boots.

27

In-hand
A lunge rope is used to teach a horse to move in a controlled way and to obey the voice of his master.

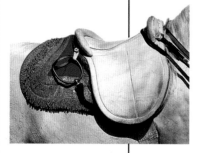

Saddle
The School has its own saddler to maintain the tack (saddles and bridles), some of which is hundreds of years old. Saddles are traditionally made out of white deerskin.

The First Chief Rider decided to train Favory himself. He wanted to get the best out of Favory without harming his unique character.

For the first two weeks, the First Chief Rider led Favory gently by hand. Then he began training Favory on the end of a long rope called a lunge.

Favory was still quite frisky, but soon he was ready to have a saddle put on his back. Favory hated the saddle, so the First Chief Rider began by putting it on for a few minutes at a time. Finally, after three months, Favory let the First Chief Rider get into the saddle and ride him.

Favory was now ready to learn how to concentrate his energy into performing the difficult dressage steps.

Favory was a fast learner. Soon, he was good enough to perform in the dressage section of the School's sell-out shows.

The First Chief Rider was pleased with his pupil's progress. Now it was time for the hardest task of all – it was time to teach Favory the Airs.

Back view
Lipizzaners' tails are often plaited for performances.

Levade
(Lev-ard)
The horse raises his front legs up to two metres off the ground.

Courbette
(Caw-bet)
This involves jumping forwards in the Levade position.

The Airs must be performed with perfect skill and grace and Favory had to work hard.

The first Air he learnt was the *Levade*. He had to rear up and balance on his hind legs.

Horses then go on to learn either the *Courbette* or the *Capriole*. Favory's lively personality made him ideally suited to the *Capriole*.

To perform this spectacular Air, Favory had to leap right off the ground and kick his back legs out behind him.

Favory practised the Airs until he was perfect, but could he keep his head in front of an audience?

During each show, the First Chief Rider presented one stallion to demonstrate the *Capriole*. It had to be a stallion of great talent.

"Let's go," said the First Chief Rider one evening to the stallion that he had chosen.

The audience gasped as a magnificent white horse trotted gracefully to the centre of the arena.

It was Favory. At last he had the chance to show off his skills. He performed the Airs to perfection and the audience loved him. Here was a real star. ❖

Capriole
(Cap-ree-ol)
This movement was developed for army horses to scare their enemies on the battlefield. It is often done in performance on a lunge rope.

Royal drum horse

"We'll call him Paddy," said the farmer's wife. "After all, he was born on St Patrick's Day."

Her five children leant over the fence to get a better look at the newborn foal in their field in Ireland. He had a beautiful brown and white coat and looked up at them with big dark eyes.

British Isles
Paddy came from Ireland, a country that is famous for horse breeding.

It was the early 1960s. In a couple of years, Paddy grew up into a fine, strong horse who enjoyed joining in the children's games – even the noisy ones. Their favourite game was to march with Paddy in procession, banging toy drums.

Skewbald
Paddy's coat was a mixture of brown and white. This kind of colouring on a horse is called skewbald.

When Paddy was old enough to start work, he was sold and taken to Edinburgh in Scotland. He began a new life pulling a milk cart for milkman Willie Wilson.

Holyroodhouse
The queen stayed here rather than Edinburgh Castle because the castle is draughty and uncomfortable.

Holyroodhouse was one of the places where they made milk deliveries. This is where Queen Elizabeth stayed on royal visits to Scotland's capital city.

One morning, Willie found their
milk route blocked by a royal parade,
which was as noisy as it was colourful.

He grabbed hold of Paddy's reins
in case the parade frightened him, but
Paddy didn't move a single muscle.
Not even when the big drums passed
just in front of his nose. Boom! Boom!

"Look, Paddy, there's the
queen," whispered Willie, spotting
who was in the big car at the back
of the procession.

A short time later, an amazing
message arrived from the Household
Cavalry, the queen's bodyguard.

A colonel of the Cavalry had
spotted Paddy standing quietly by.

Not many horses would have reacted so calmly during such a noisy procession. The colonel thought Paddy would make an ideal parade horse.

Paddy was soon on his way to the Royal Mews stables at Buckingham Palace in London to meet his new trainer, Corporal Barry McKie of the Life Guards.

Life Guard
The Life Guards are part of the Household Cavalry. They wear white horsehair plumes in their helmets.

New home
Household Cavalry horses live in stables in central London. They go to the Royal Mews for special occasions.

Drum beats
When the army fought on horseback, drums were used to send messages and raise spirits. Now Drum Horses only take part in royal parades.

Foot reins
A Drum Horse is steered by reins attached to his rider's feet. The rider needs his hands free for drumming.

The Life Guards gave Paddy a new name, Cicero. He began the months of training that would turn him into a Royal Drum Horse.

On parade days, it would be his job to walk at the head of the procession carrying two big drums.

No wonder the Life Guards needed a horse that didn't mind about noise!

Cicero's first appearance in public was on the queen's birthday in 1969. Thousands of people crowded the streets around Buckingham Palace. Cicero stayed calm as he led the procession up Horse Guard's Parade.

Cicero went on to be one of the longest serving Royal Drum Horses, retiring after ten years in 1979. ❖

Priceless
The Guards' silver drums date from 1830. They weigh 53 kilograms (118 pounds).

Celebration
The queen's birthday parade is called the Trooping of the Colour. The queen takes a salute from her troops, then leads them to Buckingham Palace up Horse Guard's Parade.

Great Britain
Red Rum was born in Ireland but ran his first ever race at Liverpool in England.

Horse auction
At an auction, buyers bid against each other for the horse they want. An auctioneer controls the bidding until a price is reached.

The favourite

"Come on boy!" shouted Tim Molony over the clamour of horses' hooves.

It was Liverpool, 1966. Molony was watching Red Rum, the young horse he had recently bought, running in his very first race.

Red Rum had got off to a bad start, but was now gaining on the leaders. Could he catch them?

Molony had bought the Irish-born bay colt at auction for well under the asking price. Molony knew he'd got a good deal but the question was, how good?

As the race entered its final stretch, Red Rum speeded up towards the leading horse. His powerful legs pushed him towards the winning post faster and faster. With his last stride, he crossed the finishing line in joint first place.

In the next few years Red Rum had many more wins and several new owners.

At Ripon in Yorkshire he was looked after by a kind stable girl. She gave him his favourite treats – peppermints and carrots – whenever he ran well.

But the stable girl soon noticed that her "Rummy" had a terrible problem. He had a serious bone disease in his hooves that could mean the end of his racing career.

Mum and Dad
Red Rum was a Thoroughbred, a breed famous for speed. His dam (mother) was called Ma*red* and his sire (father) was called Quo*rum*, hence Red Rum.

Red Rum (left) dead heats with Curlicue in his first appearance on the race track.

Diseased
The underside of Red Rum's hoof was riddled with bone disease. This made him lame, which meant that he walked with a limp.

In 1972 the injured horse was sold to trainer Ginger McCain who had stables at Southport, on the coast of north-west England.

Red Rum had seemed fit when Ginger bought him. But on his first day out on the beach with the other horses and riders, Ginger realized that something was wrong.

"I've bought a lame horse!" he shouted. "Get him into the sea. We'll try saltwater on his legs."

What happened next saved Red Rum's career.

As Red Rum came out of the sea he seemed to be moving more easily.

"Look, he's trotting sound," said Ginger with a wide grin.

Running on the sand and cooling off in the sea was the perfect treatment for Red Rum's problem.

By the next spring, the once-lame horse was fit for the most challenging horse race of all, the Grand National.

Sand and sea
The salty sea water cleaned and cooled Red Rum's injured feet. He loved to run on sand because it was level and unchanging.

Red Rum (in front) goes for a run on Southport Sands.

Race course
The National is run at Aintree, near Liverpool, in April of every year. The race is 7 kilometres (4.5 miles) long.

In 1973, thirty-eight runners lined up at the start of the Grand National, the world's most demanding horse race. The ground was "firm", just as Red Rum preferred it.

Suddenly, they were away. Thirty-eight powerful animals galloped at top speed towards the first fence.

Becher's Brook
There are 30 big fences to jump in the National. Becher's Brook is 2 metres (6 feet) high.

In homes all over Britain, millions of television viewers settled down to enjoy the annual race.

Crisp took an early lead, with Red Rum back in twelfth place.

Red Rum gradually crept up the field, until, soaring over a fence, he found himself in second place.

Crisp and Red Rum were now a long way ahead of the chasing pack.

"And it's Crisp, Crisp in the lead from Red Rum, but Red Rum is making ground on him!" shouted the commentator excitedly.

Most horses would have settled for second place, but not Red Rum. Crisp was beginning to tire and, with each enormous stride, Red Rum was catching him.

"Red Rum! It's Red Rum! Red Rum has snatched it from Crisp!" shouted the commentator, as Red Rum flashed past the finishing post in first place.

Photo finish
The National tests not only a horse's speed and jumping ability but also its stamina, or strength to keep going. At the end of the race, there is a long, hard gallop to the finishing post.

First prize
The prize for winning the Grand National was a gold cup and more than £25,000.

Statue
A statue of Red Rum was made for Aintree, to celebrate its greatest victor. It was unveiled in 1988.

Not only had Red Rum won the Grand National, but he had set a new record time of 9 minutes, 1.9 seconds. He had run at a speed of nearly 46 kilometres per hour.

Red Rum was a national hero.

The next year Red Rum entered the race again and amazingly won it for the second time. He was runner-up in 1975 and 1976, before winning it for a staggering third time in 1977, when he was 12 years old.

No other horse has won the race three times. It is unlikely the record will ever be beaten.

Red Rum attends the unveiling of his statue.

Easy to spot
In his work as a celebrity, Red Rum always wore his famous sheepskin noseband.

A few years later, Red Rum retired from racing and began a new life as a celebrity. He attended the opening of supermarkets, and many other events, as a star guest.

Red Rum died in 1995 at the ripe old age of 30. He is buried in a special grave next to the winning post at Aintree, where he had his greatest triumphs. Fans from all over the world visit to pay their respects to the greatest race horse ever. ❖

Sunny shadow
On sunny days, the shadow of the winning post at Aintree falls on Red Rum's grave.

RED RUM
3RD MAY 1965
18TH OCTOBER 1995
Grand National Record
1973 - Winner
1974 - Winner
1975 - Second
1976 - Second
1977 - Winner

The horse family

Horses and ponies belong to the same family as donkeys, wild asses and zebras. This is called the Equid (Eck-wid) family.

In the wild, horses live in herds on open grasslands. They use speed to escape from their enemies, and newborn foals can get up and run within an hour of being born.

Horses form strong bonds with other members of their herd. This loyalty is easily transferred to a human owner.

Hands high
The height of a horse is measured in "hands". One hand is the width of an adult's hand – about 10 centimetres (4 inches).

Donkey

Wild ass

Zebra

Domestic horses come in many shapes and sizes, but there are three main types – heavy horses, light horses and ponies. Heavy horses are the largest and can measure over 168 centimetres (67 inches) high. Ponies are the smallest and measure under 147 centimetres (58 inches).

The oldest breed of horse is the Przewalski (perz-uh-vol-skee) horse, which comes from Mongolia in Asia. It is the only living link with the wild ancestors of today's horses and ponies. ❖

Przewalski horses

Heavy horse
Heavy horses are tall and have broad, strong shoulders.

Light horse
Light horses have narrow bodies, long legs and sloped shoulders.

Pony
Ponies have shorter legs in relation to their bodies than light and heavy horses.

47

Glossary

Ambush
A surprise attack made from a hiding place.

Arena
An enclosed space for large shows and sporting events.

Bay
A horse with a reddish coat and black mane, tail, legs, ears and nose.

Ceremonial occasion
A special event during which a series of acts are performed.

Chasing pack
The group of horses behind the leaders in a horse race.

Colt
A young male horse.

Continent
One of the Earth's large land masses, e.g., Africa or Asia.

Cowboy
A person who works with cattle on a ranch.

Dam
The female parent of an animal, especially a horse.

Dead heat
A tie for first place in a race between two or more contestants.

Film studio
A company that makes films.

Foal
A young horse.

Gorge
A deep valley, often with a river running through it.

Groom
A person who looks after horses.

Lame
Having an injured leg or foot that causes a limp. Limping is walking unevenly.

Mare
A fully grown female horse.

Mews
A yard or street lined with stables.

Palomino
A horse with a gold-coloured coat and a white mane and tail.

Parade
A procession of people, and often a band, to celebrate a special occasion.

Quicksand
A deep, wet bed of sand that sucks down anything on its surface.

Relay
A system where fresh runners or horses are posted at intervals along a route. Each member of a relay team runs only one part of the route.

Runner-up
The person or horse that finishes second in a race or competition.

Sire
The male parent of an animal, especially a horse.

Stagecoach
A horse-drawn passenger coach that travels along a regular route.

Stallion
A fully grown male horse that can be used for breeding.

Telegraph
A system for sending messages over long distances. It uses electronic signals sent through a wire.

Trek
A long and often difficult journey.

Trotting sound
To run slowly and smoothly without limping.

Western
A film about cowboys in the western United States, especially during the time of exploration.

White House
The large white building in Washington, DC, that is home to the president of the United States.